JEWLISH BY JAMIE

One People. Many Flavors.

JAMIE GELLER WITH DANA & JACOB ATTIAS

Feldheim Publishers
Jerusalem-New York
© 2020 by Kosher Network
International, LLC and
Jamie Geller Photographs

Feldheim Publishers
POB 43163, Jerusalem,
Israel, 91431
208 Airport Executive Park,
Nanuet, NY 10954
feldheim.com
koshernetwork.com

ISBN 978-1-68025-126-5

Printed in China

Photography:
Jacob and Dana Attias

Additional Photography:
Andrew Purcell,
Nimrod Saunders, Atara Whitman

Editor: Tamar Genger

Contents

7 CHALLAH

27 DIPS

39 VEGETABLES

57 CHEESE

77 FISH

89 MEAT

109 HOLIDAYS

135 DESSERT

We know what you're thinking,

your grandmother's recipes are better. Yes, we've heard it all before. But since you'll never get the exact ingredients from her ("a pinch of this, a scoop of that"), you might as well dive right in.

The reason grandmothers never reveal their recipes is because they don't use recipes. They cook with their senses. They know if challah dough needs more flour just by its feel.

There's the Yiddish word potchke that means "to mess around," or "to waste time and effort." Apparently, our grandparents had plenty of time to potchke around in the kitchen, keep fish in the bathtub, and peel tomatoes by hand. For us with our kids, careers and carpools, it's hard to find time to get to know our challah dough in the same way. So, with the desire and struggle to recreate the flavors that came out of our grandparent's kitchens - where do we even begin?

Eating a meal from the pages of this book is not just eating a meal. Every meal is a reflection of the world. Each bite is composed of cultures and history, land and people. Thousands of years of battles, and different religions pepper each mouthful.

At the heart of this recipe collection are simple ingredients with big, sunny, explosive flavors. Each bite is a deep dive into food and faith, inspired by the wandering Jew. Simultaneously ancient and modern our recipes hail from The Middle East, the Far East, North Africa, North America and everywhere around and in-between. We extend our warmest invitation to taste the many, many, many foods and flavors of our people.

CHALLAH

חלה
['Hallah' – with a hard h]

BRAIDING A 6 STRAND CHALLAH

BRAIDING A 2 STRAND CHALLAH

ZAHTAR & OLIVE STUFFED CHALLAH

CHALLAH IN A BAG

PRETZEL CHALLAH

GARLIC STUFFED CHALLAH KNOTS

CINNAMON ROLL CHALLAH

HONEY WHOLE-WHEAT CHALLAH

APPLE CHALLAH

how to braid a
6 STRAND
CHALLAH

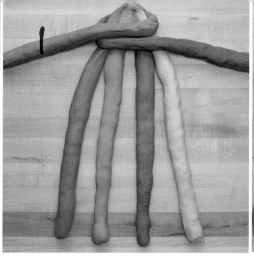

Cross the left and
right strands.

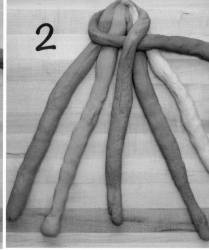

Top left into
the middle.

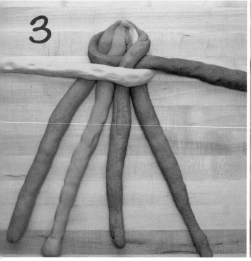

Second from right
goes over.

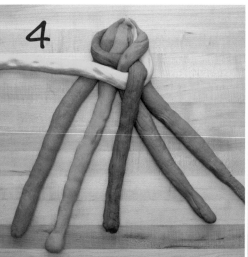

Top right into
the middle.

Second from left
goes over.

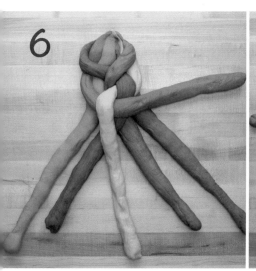

Top left into
the middle.

Second from right
goes over.

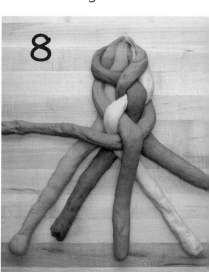

Top right into
the middle.

Repeat steps 5 - 8 until you reach the end...

how to braid a
2 STRAND CHALLAH

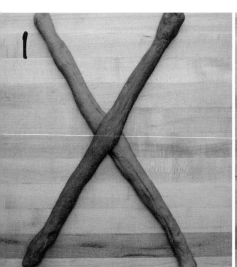

1

Cross the strands.

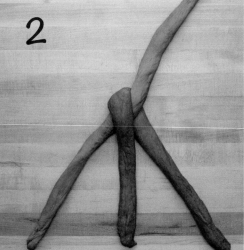

2

Top left into the middle.

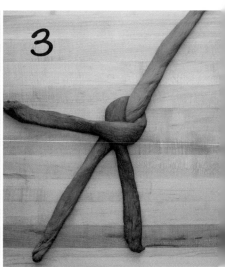

3

Second from right goes over.

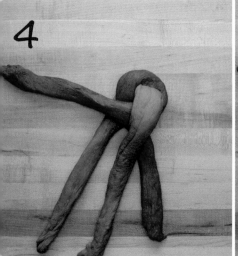

4

Top right into the middle.

5

Second from left goes over.

6

Top left into the middle.

Repeat steps 3 - 6 until you reach the end...

Second from right
goes over.

Top right into
the middle.

Second from left
goes over.

Top left into
the middle.

Second from right
goes over.

Pinch the
ends together

Zahtar & Olive Stuffed Challah

Classy on the outside, party on the inside.

Makes: 1 large challah

DOUGH
¾ cup warm water
**2¼ teaspoons active
 dry yeast (1 packet)**
3 tablespoons sugar
**2 tablespoons
 vegetable oil**
1 large egg
1 teaspoon salt
3 cups all-purpose flour

FILLING
3 tablespoons olive oil
3 tablespoons za'atar
½ cup sliced olives

TOPPING
1 egg
Za'atar

א In a large bowl, use a fork to mix the warm water, yeast, sugar, vegetable oil, egg and salt. Gradually add the flour and mix until a dough forms. When the dough is too dense to mix, use your hands.

ב On a floured surface, knead until the dough becomes soft and smooth, about 5 to 10 minutes. Place the dough in a bowl, cover and rise in a warm part of the kitchen until it doubles in size, at least 1 hour.

ג Separate the dough into 3 even pieces. Use a rolling pin to flatten the first piece of dough into a 9 by 9 inch square. Spread 1 tablespoon of olive oil then sprinkle za'atar and some sliced olives. Roll it up and pinch the ends. Repeat for the other two pieces of dough. Stretch the strands to 12 inches in length. Braid and transfer to a non-stick baking tray.

ד Brush with a beaten egg. Rise in a warm part of the kitchen for 45 minutes. Preheat the oven to 350°F / 175°C.

ה Brush with more egg and sprinkle with za'atar. Bake for 30 minutes. The challah is done when you tap the bottom of the loaf and it makes a hollow sound.

> ## TIP
> For a classic challah recipe, use this recipe without the filling. Simply braid and sprinkle with sesame or poppy seeds instead.

Challah
in a
Bag

a.k.a. the lazy man's challah.
It's as easy as aleph, bet, gimmel.

Makes: 1 large challah

DOUGH
2¼ teaspoons active dry yeast (1 packet)
¾ cup warm water
3 tablespoons sugar
1½ teaspoons salt
⅓ cup vegetable oil
3 cups all-purpose flour

TOPPING
1 egg (for vegan challah, substitute olive oil)
Sesame seeds

א In a 1 gallon ziplock bag, add the yeast, water, sugar, salt, oil and flour. Zip it closed.

ב Squeeze the dough in the bag until all the ingredients are evenly mixed, about 5 minutes. Kids are especially good at this step!

ג Fill a large bowl with warm water from the sink. Place the bag in the bowl to rise for 1 hour.

ד Separate the dough into 3 even pieces. On a floured surface, roll them out into strands. If there are any clumps of flour in the dough, knead them out. Braid and transfer to a non-stick baking tray.

ה Preheat oven to 350°F / 175°C. Brush the challah with a beaten egg (or olive oil) and sprinkle with sesame seeds. Let the challah rise for 45 minutes.

ו Brush with egg (or olive oil) again and sprinkle with more sesame seeds. Bake for 25-30 minutes until golden. The challah is done when you tap the bottom of the loaf and it makes a hollow sound.

TIP
You're done squeezing the bag when there are no clumps of flour left in the dough.

▶ watch video

Pretzel & Challah - a match made in heaven.

Makes: 2 small challahs

DOUGH
2¼ teaspoons active dry yeast (1 packet)
¾ cup warm water
3 tablespoons `sugar
2 tablespoons vegetable oil
1 large egg
1 teaspoon salt
3 cups all-purpose flour

PRETZEL
4 cups boiling water
½ cup baking soda

TOPPING
1 egg
Coarse pretzel salt

א In a large bowl, use a fork to mix the yeast, warm water, sugar, oil, egg and salt. Gradually add the flour and mix until a dough forms. When the dough is too dense to mix, use your hands.

ב On a floured surface, knead until the dough becomes soft and smooth, about 5 to 10 minutes. Place the dough in a bowl, cover and rise in a warm part of the kitchen until it doubles in size, at least 1 hour.

ג Place the dough on the counter and cut it in half. Cut each half into 3 even pieces. Roll them out into strands and braid two separate challahs.

ד For this step (we call it 'pretzelfication'), bring 4 cups of water to a boil. Pour it into a large casserole dish. Add the baking soda and mix with a fork until it is completely dissolved.

ה Gently place the challahs into the water for 15 seconds on each side, one challah at a time, using a spatula to carefully flip. Remove the challahs directly onto a baking sheet.

ו Preheat the oven to 375°F / 190°C. Let the challahs rise for 30 minutes.

ז Brush the challahs with an egg yolk and sprinkle generously with coarse pretzel salt. Bake for 15 minutes. The challah is done when you tap the bottom of the loaf and it makes a hollow sound.

> **TIP**
> You can make one big challah instead of two small ones but baking time depends on the size of the challah so a bigger challah should bake for 18 to 20 mins.

Pretzel Challah

Makes: 10 challah knots

DOUGH
1 large egg
⅓ cup olive oil
1¾ cups warm water
**4½ teaspoons active
    dry yeast (2 packets)**
⅓ cup sugar
1 tablespoon salt
7 cups all-purpose flour

FILLING
⅓ cup olive oil
8 cloves garlic, sliced
Parsley flakes

TOPPING
1 egg
4 cloves garlic, chopped
Parsley flakes
Kosher salt

א In a large bowl, use a fork to mix the egg, oil, water, yeast, sugar and salt. Gradually add the flour and mix until a dough forms. When the dough is too dense to mix, use your hands.

ב On a floured surface, knead until the dough becomes soft and smooth, about 5 to 10 minutes. Place the dough in a bowl, cover and rise in a warm part of the kitchen until it doubles in size, at least 1 hour.

ג Meanwhile, cook the olive oil and sliced garlic over medium-low heat for about 4 minutes or until lightly golden. Set aside.

ד Split the dough into 10 evenly-sized pieces. Use a rolling pin to flatten the first piece of dough into a square. Spread a spoonful of oil and garlic on the dough. Roll up each strand and pinch the ends. Stretch with your hands then twist into a simple knot.

ה Place the rolls on a baking tray and cover with a towel. Let them rise for 30 minutes. Preheat the oven to 425°F / 220°C.

ו Brush the rolls with a beaten egg and sprinkle the chopped garlic, parsley and salt on top.

ז Bake for 8 to 15 minutes or until golden.

Garlic Stuffed
Challah Knots

▶ watch video

Cinnamon Roll Challah

Let's get rollin'.

Makes: 1 large challah

DOUGH
3½ cups all-purpose flour
2 large eggs
2¼ teaspoons active dry yeast (1 packet)
3 tablespoons honey
⅓ cup olive oil
1 teaspoon salt
⅔ cup warm water

FILLING
⅓ cup canola oil
¾ cup brown sugar
1½ teaspoons cinnamon
⅛ teaspoon salt

TOPPING
1 egg
Coarse sugar, optional

> **TIP**
> You can use a bowl too, but this is way more fun!

▶ watch video

א Place the flour in the center of a large surface. Make a "bowl" in the middle of the flour like a crater in the top of a pyramid (see photo).

ב In the "bowl" add the eggs, yeast, honey, oil, salt and half of the water. Mix with a fork. Use your hands to mix some of the flour from the edges into the center. Add the other half of the water while there is still a bowl shape. Mix into a dough and knead for 5 to 10 minutes until smooth.

ג Cover with a towel and rise until the dough has doubled in size, at least 1 hour.

ד While the dough is rising, make the filling. In a small bowl, mix together the oil, brown sugar, cinnamon and salt.

ה Separate the dough into 3 even pieces. Use a rolling pin to flatten the first piece of dough into a 9 by 9 inch square. Spread ⅓ of the cinnamon mixture on top, leaving 1 inch of space around the edges. Roll it up and pinch the ends. Repeat for the other two pieces of dough. Stretch the strands to 12 inches in length. Braid and transfer to a non-stick baking tray.

ו Brush with a beaten egg. Let it rise for 45 minutes. Preheat the oven to 375°F / 190°C.

ז Gently brush again with egg and sprinkle with coarse sugar. Bake for 30 minutes. If the challah is getting too dark, place a piece of aluminum foil on top. The challah is done when you tap the bottom of the loaf and it makes a hollow sound.

Honey Whole Wheat Challah

So healthy - you can eat the "whole" thing.

Makes: 1 large challah

DOUGH
1 cup warm water
2¼ teaspoons active dry yeast (1 packet)
⅓ cup honey
1 large egg
¼ cup olive oil
1 teaspoon salt
3½ cups of whole wheat flour

TOPPING
1 egg
Seeds (pumpkin, sesame, poppy)

א In a large bowl, use a fork to mix the warm water, yeast, honey, egg, oil and salt. Gradually add the flour and mix until a dough forms. When the dough is too dense to mix, use your hands.

ב On a floured surface, knead until the dough becomes soft and smooth, about 5 to 10 minutes. Place the dough in a bowl, cover and rise in a warm part of the kitchen until it doubles in size, at least 1 hour.

ג Separate the dough into 3 even pieces and roll them out into strands. Braid and transfer to a non-stick baking tray.

ד Cover with a towel and place in a warm area to rise for about 1 hour, until it looks light and airy. Preheat oven to 350°F / 175°C.

ה Brush with 1 beaten egg and sprinkle with seeds. Bake for 30 minutes. The challah is done when you tap the bottom of the loaf and it makes a hollow sound.

Apple Challah

Originally a top-secret recipe by Cindy, Jacob's mom.
Now tried and tested by millions of Jewlish by Jamie fans.

Makes: 1 large challah

DOUGH

2¼ teaspoons active dry yeast (1 packet)
1 cup warm water
⅓ cup sugar
2 large eggs
1¼ teaspoons salt
⅓ cup vegetable oil
⅛ teaspoon sesame oil
3¾ cups all-purpose flour + ¼ more for dusting

FILLING

1 large granny smith apple, thinly sliced
3 tablespoons sugar
1 teaspoon ground cinnamon

TOPPING

1 egg
Coarse sugar

▶ watch video

א In a large bowl, use a fork to mix the yeast, warm water, sugar, eggs, salt, vegetable oil and sesame oil. Gradually add the flour and mix until a dough forms. When the dough is too dense to mix, use your hands.

ב Transfer the dough to a floured surface and knead for 5 minutes - it should be a little sticky. Place the dough in a bowl, cover and rise in a warm part of the kitchen until it doubles in size, at least 1 hour.

ג On a floured surface, roll out the dough into a rectangle about 10 inches wide and 14 inches long. Trim the edges to shape it into a rectangle.

ד Place a line of apple slices ⅓ of the way from the bottom of the rectangle (see photo). There should be enough space below the apples to fold the dough over them. Sprinkle 1 tablespoon of sugar and ⅓ teaspoon of cinnamon over the apples. Fold the dough over and repeat two more times. There may only be enough space for 2 rows of apples, and that's okay. If there is any extra dough at the top, fold it over the rest of the roll.

ה Cut the roll into 8 sections. Place each section in a greased bundt pan long-ways (see photo). Place an apple slice between each section. Brush with egg and sprinkle with coarse sugar.

ו Let the challah rest for an hour. Preheat the oven to 350° / 175°. Bake for 30-35 minutes until golden.

DIPS

ממרח
[Mimrah] – literally
translates to 'spread'

BABA GANOUSH

HUMMUS

TAHINI WITH MINT

MATBUCHA

VEGETARIAN CHOPPED LIVER

Baba Ganoush

In Israel, "baba" is often called salat hazilim (eggplant salad) or hazilim b'tchina (eggplant in tahini). In Arabic, baba ganoush translates to "pampered daddy".

This mezze dip is best when it is very smoky, a characteristic that doesn't come with the store-bought variety. Take care to wrap the eggplants well, so you can blast them with fire without making a mess. Some eggplants have slightly bitter seeds, so taste them after you peel off the burnt eggplant skin. Sometimes they're delicious and should be included. Also, while garlic is traditionally included in baba, this recipe is great without since it's already so smoky and flavorful.

Serves 6

**2 medium-sized
   eggplants**
½ cup of raw tahini
**1 tablespoon lemon
   juice**
**2 cloves crushed garlic
   (optional)**
¼ teaspoon salt

א With a fork, prick a couple of holes in the eggplants. Wrap each eggplant in two layers of aluminum foil. Place them directly on a stovetop flame on medium heat for about 20 minutes, rotating every 5 minutes, until they smell very smoky. Or, you can use a grill and skip the foil.

ב Allow the eggplants to cool.

ג Over the sink, unwrap the foil and place the eggplants in a strainer. Peel off the skin with your hands and cut them in half. Some liquid will drain out into the sink. Remove the seeds (optional - sometimes eggplant seeds taste bitter).

ד Place the eggplants in a bowl. Add raw tahini, lemon juice, garlic and salt.

ה Mash with a fork. If it's too liquidy, add more raw tahini. Taste and adjust lemon and salt to your preference.

▶ watch video

Hummus

Serves 8

2 cups dried chickpeas
1 teaspoon baking soda
1 onion, peeled
⅔ cup raw tahini
⅓ cup lemon juice,
  about 2 large lemons
2 cloves garlic, crushed
2 teaspoons salt

TOPPINGS
Zahtar
Olive oil
Paprika
Boiled egg, quartered
Chopped parsley
1 onion, quartered

א Place the chickpeas in a large bowl with ½ teaspoon of baking soda. Cover the chickpeas with cold water and soak overnight (at least 8 hours).

ב Drain the chickpeas, rinse and place in a large pot. Cover with water that goes 2 inches over the chickpeas. Add ½ teaspoon of baking soda along with the peeled onion.

ג Cover and cook on medium heat until the chickpeas are soft enough to easily smush between two fingers. This takes about an hour and a half.

ד Strain the chickpeas and transfer to a blender or food processor. Set some chickpeas aside for garnishing. You can add the onion to the food processor too.

ה Add the tahini, lemon juice, garlic, 2 tablespoons of water and salt. Blend. You may need to scrape down the sides. Add more water, one tablespoon at a time, until it reaches a creamy consistency. Note that warm hummus will thicken as it cools down. Adjust salt to taste.

Tip: Small chickpeas make smoother, tastier hummus.
Tip: Use Israeli tahini if possible - a high quality tahini makes a silky-smooth hummus.
Pro-tip: Save the liquid from the chickpeas to use as a soup stock.

Tahini with Mint

Use this dip for everything - dipping bread, dressing salad or drizzling on fish. Tahini is a lifestyle.

Serves 6

1 cup mint leaves (bitter stems removed)
½ cup raw tahini
2 tablespoons lemon juice
½ teaspoon salt
6 tablespoons water
1 clove garlic, peeled

א Add all the ingredients to a blender or food processor.

ב Blend until it reaches a smooth consistency.

ג Adjust salt to taste.

> **TIP**
> Shake and mix your jar of raw tahini before using. The oil tends to rise to the top and the sesame sinks to the bottom.

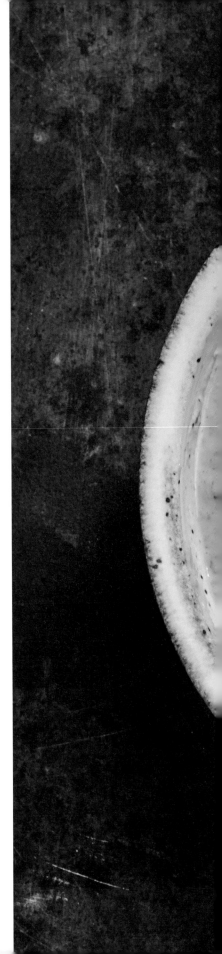

▶ watch video

Matbucha

Serves 6

2 red bell peppers
1 chili pepper, if you like
   the heat
2 cans peeled diced
   tomatoes, 14.5 oz
   (410 g) each

5 cloves garlic, sliced
1 tablespoon sugar
4 tablespoons olive
   oil
1 teaspoon salt
1 tablespoon paprika

א Place the chili and bell peppers on a baking sheet in the oven. Broil for 20 minutes, flipping after 10. The peppers should be blackened on all sides. Once cool, remove the blackened skin from the peppers. Cut each pepper in half and remove the seeds and stems, or keep some seeds for a spicier dish. Cut the peppers into strips and set aside.

ב While the peppers are cooking, add the canned tomatoes, sliced garlic and sugar to a pot. Cook on medium heat stirring occasionally until it reaches a jam-like consistency, about 20 minutes.

ג Add the olive oil and sliced peppers to the pot. Cook on medium-low heat for 1 hour, stirring occasionally to prevent it from sticking to the bottom of the pan.

ד Add the salt and paprika. Stir and allow to cool before serving.

> **TIP**
> Prepare 1 day in advance.
> Matbucha tastes even
> better after 1-2 days.

Vegetarian Chopped Liver

Serves 8

1 cup whole walnuts
4 tablespoons vegetable oil
2 onions, chopped
1 cup chopped mushrooms, 10 oz (280 g)
4 eggs, boiled
3 sprigs of parsley
½ teaspoon salt
¼ teaspoon ground black pepper

א Toast the walnuts in a frying pan on medium heat for 2 minutes, stirring often. Remove the walnuts and set aside.

ב Add 2 tablespoons of the oil to the pan and fry the onions on medium-low heat until golden and caramelized, about 20 minutes.

ג Add 2 tablespoons of oil to a second frying pan and cook the mushrooms on medium heat until soft, about 10 minutes.

ד Add the toasted walnuts to a food processor and grind to a powder. Then, add the onions, mushrooms, boiled eggs, walnuts, parsley, salt and pepper. Grind to your desired consistency. Taste and adjust salt if necessary.

ה Garnish with chopped parsley, chopped hard-boiled egg or sliced red onion.

VEGETABLES

ירקות
[Ye-ra-kote] – similar to the
Hebrew word for green, "yarok"

MEDITERRANEAN PTITIM SALAD

CAULIFLOWER-RICE TABBOULEH

SALAD

COUSCOUS SALAD WITH

POMEGRANATE CHICKEN

SPICY NORTH AFRICAN CARROT

SALAD

SABICH

BORSCHT

DILL PICKLES

GADI'S ISRAELI PICKLES

Mediterranean Ptitim Salad

In the 1950s, only a few years after the state of Israel was established, the Israeli population had doubled and food was in short supply. So they did what Israelis do best – invent something new. As a cheap substitute for rice, ptitim were born! Ptitim have come a long way since then, making appearances in upscale restaurants. Internationally, ptitim are now known as "Israeli couscous" or "pearl couscous".

Serves 6

1½ cups ptitim
1 teaspoon olive oil
½ teaspoon cumin
1¾ cups water
1 cup cherry tomatoes, halved
½ cup mint, chopped
½ cup parsley, chopped
½ red onion, chopped
2 pickled artichoke hearts, quartered
Goat feta, crumbled

TOPPING
Juice of ½ lemon
1 tablespoon olive oil
½ teaspoon date honey (known as "silan" in Hebrew, or substitute regular honey)
Salt and pepper, to taste

א Add ptitim to a pot on medium heat with the olive oil and cumin. Stir and cook for 1 minute. Add the water, bring to a boil and cover on low heat for 12 minutes.

ב Wait a few minutes for the ptitim to cool then add them to your salad bowl with the tomatoes, mint, parsley, red onion, artichoke hearts and feta.

ג Mix the lemon juice, olive oil, date honey, salt and pepper in a small bowl. Pour over the salad. It doesn't need much salt because of the feta cheese.

ד Toss gently and serve at room temperature.

► watch video

Cauliflower-Rice Tabbouleh Salad

▶ watch video

Originating in the moutain range between Syria and Lebanon, tabbouleh is now popular in Israel and throughout the Middle East. This version uses cauliflower rice, which has become super "duper" trendy, and is a delicious gluten-freee substituion for the bulgur wheat. Serve this on a hot day along with hummus, baba ganoush and bread for dipping. Jewish families in Syria used to serve tabbouleh salad with romaine leaves for scooping it up.

Serves 4

½ **small cauliflower**
2 **cups of flat-leaf parsley, finely chopped (approx. 3 bunches)**
½ **cup of mint, finely chopped**
1 **Persian cucumber, chopped (the normal kind in Israel)**
1 **cup cherry tomatoes, quartered**
½ **small white onion, chopped**
¼ **cup quality extra virgin olive oil**
3 **tablespoons lemon juice**
½ **teaspoon kosher salt**
¼ **teaspoon freshly cracked black pepper**
¼ **teaspoon cumin**

א Cut the cauliflower in half, cut out the core, and cut into chunks.

ב Place the cauliflower into a food processor. Pulse about 5 times or until the pieces are the size of rice grains. You can also use a hand grater for this step.

ג Treansfer the cauliflower to a microwavable bowl. Microwave for 2½ minutes.

TABBOULEH SALAD:

Literally just add everything to a bowl and mix.

Tip 1: It's all about the parsley. Fresh parsley is traditionally the main ingredient in tabbouleh salad.

Tip 2: Make sure the parsley and mint are dry before adding them to the salad. Extra water in the salad dilutes the flavor.

Couscous Salad with Pomegranate Chicken

Serves 4

CHICKEN

2 chicken breasts, cubed

1 tablespoon harissa paste

½ cup pomegranate juice

1 tablespoon olive oil

SALAD

1 cup couscous

1 cup boiling water

½ teaspoon salt

1 cup cherry tomatoes, chopped

½ cup mint, chopped

½ cup parsley, chopped

2 tablespoons pomegranate seeds

DRESSING

1 tablespoon lemon juice

3 tablespoons extra-virgin olive oil

Salt and pepper

א Place the cubed chicken in a bowl with the harissa paste and pomegranate juice. Mix, cover with plastic wrap and marinate for 15 minutes.

ב Add 1 cup of couscous to a large bowl with 1 cup of boiiling water and ½ teaspoon of salt. Stir and cover for 10 minutes. Meanwhile, chop your vegetables. When the 10 minutes are up fluff the couscous with a fork.

ג Place a pan on medium-high heat. Once hot, add 1 tablespoon of olive oil and add the marinated chicken. Cook for 6 to 8 minutes until cooked through.

ד To serve, place the chicken on top of the couscous along with the cherry tomatoes, mint, and parsley, cilantro, and pomegranate seeds.

ה Mix the dressing ingredients in a separate bowl and pour over the salad. Sprinkle additional salt and pepper to taste.

TIP
For a vegan option, subsitute the chicken with toasted cashews and pistachios

▶ watch video

Spicy North African Carrot Salad

You're sitting at a restaurant on the Tel Aviv docks next to the gentle waves of the Mediterranean - white tablecloths, white wine, and whole roasted fish on platters. The waiter places ten different salads on the table. This is one of those salads. How did this North African salad find its way to a Tel Aviv fish restaurant? Well, that's Israel in a nutshell.

Serves 6

7 medium sized carrots
4 tablespoons olive oil
4 cloves garlic
1 teaspoon cumin
2 teaspoons paprika
Pinch of cayenne pepper
¼ teaspoon salt
1 tablespoon lemon juice
¼ cup chopped parsley or cilantro leaves

א Peel carrots and cut into ¼ inch cylinders.

ב Add carrots to a pot and cover with water. Bring to a boil and cook for 10 minutes until tender but still crisp. Strain carrots and transfer to a bowl.

ג Add olive oil to a pan on medium-low heat. Add the chopped garlic, cumin, paprika and cayenne pepper. Cook for 1 minute, stirring often. Be careful not to burn the spices.

ד Pour the mixture on top of the carrots.

ה Add the lemon juice, chopped parsley (or cilantro) and salt. Mix, taste and adjust the salt if necessary.

Sabich

Fried eggplant and hard-boiled eggs in a pita. This Jewish-Iraqi dish that was originally eaten on Shabbat mornings has become a staple of Israeli street food. Some claim that the word sabich comes from the Arabic word "sabah" which translates to "morning". The most traditional condiment that accompanies sabich is called "amba", a pickled mango sauce, which can be found in Middle Eastern and some Kosher markets.

Serves 5

5 pitas
1 medium eggplant
1 tablespoon salt
Oil, for frying

SIDES
2 potatoes, peeled
    and sliced to ¼ inch
    thickness
3 eggs, hard-boiled and
    sliced
1 bunch parsley, finely
    chopped
¼ red cabbage,
    shredded
Tahini
Salt and pepper
Amba (mango sauce)
Schug (spicy chili
    paste)
Sliced pickles

א Cut the eggplant into half-inch slices. Place the slices on a baking tray. Sprinkle the eggplant with salt on both sides. Wait 20 minutes for the salt to pull the water out of the eggplant which makes it soft. Wipe off the salt and water with a paper towel.

ב Meanwhile, bring a large pot of water to a boil. Peel and slice the potatoes. Add them to the boiling water, cover and cook for 11 minutes. This is also a good time to prepare the hard boiled eggs.

ג Add enough oil to a frying pan to cover the bottom of the pan, then bring to medium-low heat. Add the eggplant and cook on each side for 4 to 5 minutes. If the flame is too high, the eggplant will burn without cooking on the inside.

ד Remove the eggplant from the oil and place on a paper towel lined tray. Place more paper towels on top and squeeze them down with a spoon to remove the oil from the eggplant.

ה Time to stuff the pitas! Get all the sides ready and add one layer at a time. Don't forget a pinch of salt and pepper—it changes everything.

▶ **watch video**

Borscht

Tradition, tradition!

Serves 6-8

2 tablespoons vegetable oil
2 carrots, grated or finely chopped
1 large onion, grated or finely chopped
3 medium beets
2 potatoes, peeled and cubed
10 cups water
2 teaspoons sugar
Salt and pepper
Dill, for garnish
Sour cream, for garnish

א Place a large pot on medium heat and add the oil. Add the carrots and onion. Cook for 10 minutes until soft.

ב Peel the beets under gently running water to prevent your hands from turning red. Cut into small cubes or matchsticks.

ג Add the beets and potatoes to the pot. Fill with 10 cups of water and simmer until the beets are soft, about 20-25 minutes.

ד Season with sugar, salt and pepper. Adjust to taste.

ה Garnish with a big dollop of sour cream and a sprig of fresh dill. Can be served hot on a snowy night or cold on a sunny summer day.

The best pickles are made at home. We recommend using Kirby cucumbers, which are the most similar to the ones you'll find in a deli. Persian cucumbers are widely available and also make classic, crunchy pickles.

Makes: 20 pickles

BRINE
1½ cups water
1 cup white vinegar, 5% acidity

FOR EACH JAR
4-5 cucumbers, depending on size
1 tablespoon kosher salt
1 small bunch of fresh dill
1 teaspoon crushed chili peppers
1 bay leaf
2 cloves of garlic, crushed

א Wash the cucumbers then cut off the ends. Slice each cucumber into 4 spears.

ב For the brine, mix together the water and white vinegar.

ג Fill a few jars with the kosher salt, dill, crushed chili peppers, bay leaf and garlic. Add the cucumber spears so they are tightly packed. Pour the brine to the top and close the jars. You don't need glass jars. Any container will work.

ד Shake to mix the ingredients then place in the fridge.

ה You can eat the pickles after 8 hours, but they are best after several days. They will keep for several weeks.

Dill
Pickles

Gadi's Israeli Pickles

Dana's uncle, Gadi, lives next to the Mahane Yehuda market in Jerusalem. He shops in the back streets of the market where the locals go to buy the "good stuff". And, by "good stuff", we're referring to the highest quality produce for the lowest price.

Serves 6-8

VEGETABLES
2 carrots
1 red pepper
1 kohlrabi
1 spicy pepper
¼ cabbage
¼ small cauliflower

BRINE
5 cups water
1½ cups vinegar
2 lemons
1 tablespoon salt
¼ teaspoon turmeric

א Wash the vegetables and cut them into chunks. "Not too thin, not too thick," as Gadi explains. Place the veggies in clean jars. You don't need the glass kind, any container will work.

ב In a pot, add the water, vinegar, salt and turmeric. Squeeze the juice from the two lemons then add in the peels. Boil for 3 minutes then remove from heat.

ג Wait 10 minutes for the brine to cool down then carefully pour into the jars.

ד Once the jars cool to room temperature, seal them and place in the fridge. Leave for two days (or a day and a half if you really can't wait).

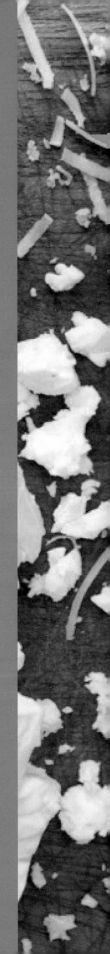

CHEESE

גבינה
[Gvina]

PITA CHIP PIZZA

BOYOS DE ESPINICA

BEET SHAKSHUKA

CREAMY SPINACH SHAKSHUKA

BOUREKAS 4-WAYS

ONE-POT CHEESY PTITIM

NOODLE KUGEL WITH JAM POKES

Pita Chip Pizza

Easy and cheesy.

Serves 3-4

3 pitas
1 tablespoon olive oil
12 oz (340 g) tomato sauce
10 oz (280 g) shredded mozzarella
3 garlic cloves, sliced
Fresh basil leaves, sliced

א Preheat oven to 375°F / 190°C.

ב Brush the pitas with olive oil on both sides.

ג Stack the pitas and slice 4 times like a pizza, so they are each cut into 8 sections. Spread out on a baking tray. Bake for 20 minutes or until golden brown.

ד Spread your favorite tomato sauce on the pita chips, followed by the mozzarella, sliced garlic and basil.

ה Bake for 5 to 10 more minutes untill the cheese is melted.

watch video

Boyos de Espinaca

There's nothing like biting into some boyos, through the crisp pastry into the cheesy filling. This recipe has been passed down among Spanish Jewry for hundreds of years, and with each and every bite, we connect with our past.

The finished boyos freeze really well, simply reheat them in the toaster or oven.

Makes: 12 pastries

DOUGH

1 cup water

1 tablespoon vegetable oil

½ teaspoon salt

3 cups flour

⅓ cup additional oil for the baking pan

FILLING

10 oz (280 g) spinach, chopped

8 oz (225 g) feta, crumbled

4 oz (115 g) Parmesan, shredded

TOPPING

Parmesan, shredded

> ## TIP
> Getting the dough thin is tricky, but practice makes perfect! The thin ner the dough, the crispier the result. Use a rolling pin to get it started, and continue the stretching by hand.

א Preheat the oven to 400°F / 200°C. Mix the water, 1 tablespoon of oil, salt and flour in a bowl. Knead until a smooth dough forms. If the dough is resisting, let it rest for 30 seconds.

ב Pour ⅓ cup oil onto a baking tray. Pinch off a small ball of dough a little larger than a golf ball. Roll the ball on the counter to make it smooth and place it in the oil. Flip so it's oiled on all sides. Repeat with all the dough.

ג For the cheese filling, mix the spinach, feta and Parmesan in a bowl.

ד Starting with the balls that were rolled first, take one, flip it in the oil and place it on a smooth surface. With a rolling pin, flatten it into a large rectangle. The dough should be paper thin when stretched to its full size. If it rips or is too difficult to flatten, let it rest for 15 minutes.

ה Add a row of the spinach mixture to the stretched out dough (see picture). Fold the bottom of the dough over the top, stretching it even thinner along the way. Fold in the sides and roll it up. Coil the roll (see picture) and tuck the end under. Place on a non-stick baking tray. Repeat with all the dough.

ו Brush with a beaten egg and sprinkle with shredded Parmesan. Bake until golden brown, about 30 to 40 minutes.

Beet Shakshuka

Serves 1-2

1 tablespoon olive oil
2 cloves garlic
1 chili pepper, minced
(optional)
½ beet, shredded
½ can diced tomatoes
(7 oz / 200 g)

5 tablespoons water
½ teaspoon salt
2 eggs
2 oz (50 g) Feta
Black pepper

א Place a pan on medium heat. Add the oil, garlic, chili pepper and beets. Cook for 5 minutes, stirring occasionally.

ב Turn the heat down to medium-low. Add the diced tomatoes, water and salt. Mix then cover for 20 minutes.

ג Mix again. With a spatula, make a little hole in the sauce and place the eggs. Sprinkle with feta cheese and fresh black pepper. Cover for 3 more minutes then check if eggs are cooked to your preference. Serve with bread for soaking up the sauce.

Creamy Spinach Shakshuka

Shakshuka is originally a Tunisian tomato-based dish. This version, with an Italian twist, has recently popped up in cafés all over Israel.

Serves 1-2

1 teaspoon butter
¼ cup onion, chopped
1 clove garlic, chopped
1 cup baby spinach
½ cup heavy cream
1 teaspoon flour
Salt and pepper
Pinch of nutmeg
2 eggs
¼ cup mozzarella,
shredded

א If using an oven-proof pan, preheat oven to broil.

ב Place your pan on the stove on medium heat. Add the butter, onion and garlic. Cook for 5 minutes until the onions start to brown.

ג Add the spinach, heavy cream, flour, salt, pepper and nutmeg. Mix.

ד Cook until sauce thickens, about 3 minutes. Stir to prevent sticking.

ה With a spatula, make a little hole in the sauce and place the eggs.

ו After the egg is comfortable in its spot, sprinkle the mozzarella.

ז If you're using an oven-proof pan, place it in the oven and broil for 3 minutes for soft yolks or until eggs are cooked to your preference. Otherwise, cover the pan, turn the heat to medium-low and cook for 3 minutes for soft yolks, or until eggs are cooked to your preference. Serve with bread for soaking up the sauce.

► watch video

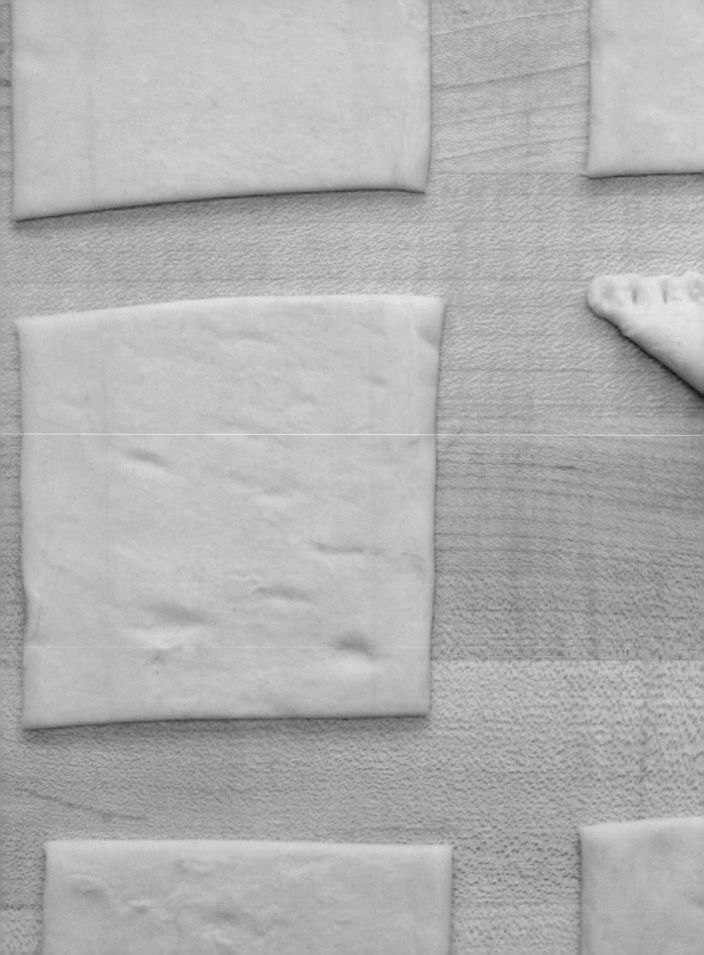

Makes: 18 bourekas

2 sheets puff pastry
2 egg yolks

CLASSIC CHEESE
1 cup feta cheese, crumbled
1 egg
1 tablespoon flour
Pinch of black pepper

MUSHROOM
1 tablespoon oil
Mushrooms, chopped
Onion, sliced
Salt & pepper

BRIE
Brie cheese

PIZZA
Tomato sauce
Mozzarella, shredded
Sliced olives

> ## TIP
> Cold pastry dough is much easier to work with, so work quickly straight out of the fridge, or return it to the fridge if it gets warm.

א Defrost the puff pastry according to the instructions on the package. Trust them. They know what's up when it comes to defrosting dough. Preheat oven to 350°F / 175°C.

ב For the *Classic Cheese Bourekas*, mix the feta, egg, flour and pepper in a bowl.

For the *Mushroom Bourekas*, add the oil, onion, mushrooms, salt and pepper to a pan on medium heat. Cook for 15 minutes, stirring occasionally, until soft.

For the *Brie Bourekas*, cut the brie into very small cubes.

For the *Pizza Bourekas*, get your tomato sauce, mozzarella and sliced olives ready.

ג Once defrosted, flour your baking surface and roll the dough out with a rolling pin into a 12x12 inch square. Make sure the dough doesn't stick to the surface.

ד Cut each sheet of dough into 9 squares. Place 1 tablespoon of your favorite filling in the center of each square and fold over into a triangle.

ה Press around the edges with a fork to seal it tightly closed. Brush with egg yolk and sprinkle with sesame seeds.

ו Bake for 30 minutes or until golden brown.

▶ watch video

Bourekas
Classic-Cheese, Mushroom, Brie and Pizza

One-Pot Cheesy Ptitim

An Italian-Israeli baby is born.

Serves 6

2 tablespoons butter
¼ cup olive oil
4 cloves garlic, sliced
¼ teaspoon crushed chili peppers
2 cups ptitim
2¼ cups water
1 cup cherry tomatoes, halved
2 cups baby spinach
1 cup Parmesan, shredded + extra for garnish
Salt and pepper
Parsley, for garnish

א Add the butter, olive oil, garlic and crushed chili peppers to a pot on medium heat. Stir and cook for 2 minutes until fragrant.

ב Add the ptitim and stir. Fry the ptitim for 1 to 2 minutes until golden-brown.

ג Add the water and stir. Cover and turn the heat down to medium-low. Simmer for 12 minutes, stirring occasionally.

ד Remove from heat and add the tomatoes, spinach, Parmesan, salt and pepper. Mix.

ה Garnish with chopped parsley and extra Parmesan.

▶ watch video

Noodle Kugel with Jam Pokes

Recipe from Mimi Linda – the queen of kugel. You can prepare this up to a day in advance and bake right before serving.

Serves 6-8

8 oz (225 g) extra-wide egg noodles
3 large eggs
⅓ cup sugar
½ cup butter, melted
8 oz (225 g) cream cheese, at room temperature
16 oz (450 g) cottage cheese
1 teaspoon vanilla
½ cup golden raisins
5 tablespoons blueberry jam
5 tablespoons apricot jam
Cinnamon

א Preheat oven to 350°F / 175°C.

ב Boil egg noodles in water for 5 to 7 minutes until al-dente. Strain.

ג Mix the eggs and sugar in a large bowl.

ד Add the butter, cream cheese, cottage cheese, vanilla and golden raisins. Mix and mash with a fork.

ה Grease an 8x8 inch baking dish. Add the strained egg noodles and the egg mixture. Gently mix. It should be quite liquidy.

ו Now we do the 'pokes'. Take a spoon and make a little hole in the kugel. With another spoon, scoop about 1 tablespoon of blueberry or apricot jam into the hole. Repeat about 9 times or until you think the kugel has enough jam. This is a top-secret kugel trick!

ז Dust the top with a thin layer of cinnamon. Bake on a low oven rack for 40 mins or until the edges are crisped to your liking.

▶ watch video

FISH

דגים
[Dag-eem]

HOMEMADE GRAVLAX

PICKLED FISH

HONEY-CARAMELIZED SALMON

WITH APPLE ARUGULA SALAD

SALMON PAELLA

MOROCCAN FISH

Homemade
Gravlax

Before buying fish for gravlax, ask if it has been commercially frozen, which means it is OK for raw consumption. You might not know it, but every piece of sushi you've ever eaten has been frozen.

Gravlax is the Scandanavian word for cured salmon. If you want to take this to the next level, which is smoked salmon, you can follow this recipe then cold-smoke it. Either way, it's delicious!

Serves 8-10 appetizer portions

2 lb (1kg) sushi-grade salmon fillet, skin on
½ cup kosher salt
¼ cup sugar
Zest of ½ a lemon
1 bunch of dill, chopped

א Place a big sheet of plastic wrap on the counter.

ב Rinse and dry the salmon. Place it on the plastic wrap. Sprinkle the salt, sugar, lemon zest and dill on the top, sides and bottom of the fish. Wrap it up.

ג Place it in a baking dish in the refrigerator (it's going to drip). Add a weight on top, such as a plate with a couple of cans on top of it (this makes the salting happen more evenly). Refrigerate for 48 hours.

ד Unwrap and rinse well. Cut thin slices with a long sharp knife.

ה Serve at brunch with bagels and cream cheese.

TIP
To find sushi-grade salmon, check a local fishmonger or Japanese market.

▶ watch video

Pickled
Fish

Serves 8-10 appetizer portions

FISH
2 trout fillets, previously frozen
½ lb (250 g) sushi-grade salmon fillet

BRINE
1½ cups water
1½ cups vinegar
¼ cup sugar
⅓ cup salt

IN THE JARS
1 head of garlic, peeled
3 teaspoons black peppercorns
3 bay leaves
1 red onion, sliced
3 tablespoons vegetable oil

א   To make the brine, add the water and vinegar to a pot and bring to a boil. Remove from heat and dissolve the sugar and salt into the water.

ב   Allow the brine to cool for 15 minutes.

ג   In each jar, add some fish, 3 cloves of garlic, a teaspoon of black peppercorns, 1 bay leaf and the slices of ¼ red onion. Don't pack the jar tightly - the fish should have room to swim.

ד   Add 1 tablespoon of vegetable oil to each jar then fill to the top with the brine. Close the jars and refrigerate for 48 hours. Serve with crackers and vodka shots.

TIP
Fresh herring is hard to find in stores, but if you can find it, use this same method.

Honey-Caramelized Salmon with Apple Arugula Salad

Apples & honey for Rosh Hashanah (and all year 'round).

Serves 4

FOR THE SALAD
1 green apple, thinly sliced
5 radishes, thinly sliced
½ tablespoon lemon juice
5 oz (140 g) arugula
1 teaspoon honey
½ tablespoon olive oil
Salt and pepper

FOR THE SALMON
4 salmon fillets (skin on or off)
Salt and pepper
4 teaspoons honey
Pinch of chili flakes
2 tablespoons olive oil (for frying)

א   Thinly slice the apple and radishes. Add to serving bowl along with the lemon juice, which prevents the apple from turning brown.

ב   Mix the honey, oil, salt and pepper in a small bowl. Immediately before serving, add arugula to the serving bowl, pour the dressing on top and toss gently.

ג   For the salmon, first dry the fillets with a paper towel. Sprinkle salt and pepper on both sides. Spread one teaspoon of honey on the side without skin. Sprinkle chili flakes.

ד   Add 2 tablespoons of olive oil to a frying pan on medium heat. Once the oil is hot, add the salmon with the skin side up (so the honey side is directly on the pan). Cook for 30 seconds then check with a spatula if the honey-glazed side is caramelized. Once caramelized, flip and cook the skin side of the salmon for 3 minutes.

watch video

Salmon Paella

Serves 6

2 tablespoons olive oil
3 cloves garlic, chopped
1 onion, finely chopped
1 red bell pepper, chopped
1 can diced tomatoes
1 teaspoon salt
1 tablespoon paprika
1 bay leaf

1 bunch green beans
3 teaspoons soup bouillon
Pinch of saffron
2½ cups water
1 cup paella rice, short-grain
1 lb (500 g) fresh salmon without skin

א Add olive oil to a wide pan on medium heat. Fry the garlic, onion and pepper until softened, about 5 minutes.

ב Add the tomatoes, salt, paprika, bay leaf and green beans. Stir and cook until the sauce starts to thicken, about 5 minutes.

ג Add the bouillon, saffron, water and rice. Stir. Simmer for 5 minutes, stirring occasionally. Add more water if the sauce goes below the surface of the rice.

ד Place the salmon slices on top and press them into the sauce. Cover the pan with foil and turn the heat to low. Cook for 15 minutes or until rice is cooked through.

▶ watch video

Moroccan Fish

This recipe hails from Tétouan, Morocco, heavily influenced by
Spanish culture, which is why this fish dish is a mash-up of garlicky Spanish
cuisine and beautifully spiced Moroccan tagine.

Serves 4

4 tablespoons olive oil
1 red bell pepper, sliced
1 chili pepper, seeds
   removed and sliced
8 cloves garlic, peeled
1 can diced tomatoes
   (14.5 oz / 400 g)
1 can cooked chickpeas
   (14.5 oz / 400g), optional
1 cup chopped cilantro
1½ cups water
½ teaspoon salt
½ teaspoon cumin
2 tablespoons + 1 teaspoon
   sweet paprika
4 fish fillets, tilapia, salmon,
   grouper or your favorite
   fish
Juice of ½ lemon

א Add 1 tablespoon of olive oil to a large pot on
medium heat. Add the peppers and cook for 10
minutes, stirring occasionally.

ב Add the garlic, diced tomatoes, chickpeas, half
of the chopped cilantro, water, salt, cumin and 1
teaspoon of paprika. Mix, cover and cook for 10
minutes.

ג Meanwhile, add 3 tablespoon of olive oil to a
large bowl. Add 2 tablespoons of paprika and a
pinch of salt, then mix. Add each piece of fish to
the mixture and flip to coat well.

ד Place the fish in the pot on top of the
vegetables and pour the remaining oil on top.
Squeeze half a lemon on top and throw in the
other half of the cilantro. Simmer until the fish is
cooked through.

ה Season with a pinch of salt and serve hot.

► watch video

MEAT

בשר
[Bahsar]

CHICKEN SOUP

MATZO BALLS

MEAT-STUFFED EGGPLANT

BRISKET

CHOLENT

ORISA

MAFRUM

HASSELBACK SALAMI

STEAK-STUFFED PITA FAJITA

Chicken Soup

Your mother and the 12th century philosopher, Maimonides, have claimed that chicken soup has healing powers. You should listen to them. This recipe is soup-er flexible, so don't worry if you don't have the exact ingredients. Throw all your favorite herbs and veggies in the broth.

Serves 8

3-4 lb (1.5 kg) whole chicken, cut up (most stores sell chicken already cut up)
4 carrots
2 onions, halved
4 celery stalks
Small bunch of fresh parsley
3 cloves garlic
3 sprigs thyme
1 bay leaf
1 tablespoon black peppercorns
1 teaspoon salt
16 cups water

א Place all the ingredients in a large pot and cover completely with cold water, about 4 quarts (16 cups). Cook uncovered on medium heat for 90 minutes. Foam will come to the top of the soup. Skim it off every so often.

ב Let's make the matzo balls while the soup cooks (see next page).

ג Use tongs to remove the chicken, carrots and celery from the pot and set aside. Pick the meat off the bones and chop the vegetables.

ד Carefully strain the broth through a strainer.

ה Add the chicken and vegetables into the soup and add salt to taste.

Matzo Balls

The super-fluffy kind.

Makes: 12 matzo balls

1 cup matzo meal
½ teaspoon salt
2 teaspoons baking powder
4 large eggs
4 tablespoons vegetable oil or schmaltz (rendered chicken fat)

א Mix the matzo meal, salt and baking powder in a large bowl.

ב In a separate bowl, gently mix the eggs and oil or schmaltz.

ג Add the egg mixture to the matzo meal mixture and gently mix until barely combined.

ד Place in the fridge until cooled, about 1 hour.

ה Bring a large pot of salted water to a boil.

ו Shape the mix into small balls.

ז Add them to the boiling water. Immediately turn the heat down to a simmer. Cover and cook for 35 minutes.

Meat Stuffed Eggplant

Serves 2-4

2 eggplants
2 tablespoons olive oil
1 onion, finely chopped
½ lb (225g) ground beef or
   lamb
¼ teaspoon cumin
Salt and pepper
1 red pepper, finely
   chopped
1 carrot, finely chopped

Tahini
4 tablespoons raw tahini
1 tablespoon lemon juice
Approx. 3 tablespoons
   water
¼ teaspoon salt, to taste

▶ watch video

א Preheat oven to 400° F / 200° C.

ב Slice the eggplants in half, lengthwise. Place cut-side up on a baking sheet and drizzle with olive oil and sprinkle with salt and pepper. Bake for 30 minutes. Some eggplants have bitter seeds, so when they're finished cooking, taste the seeds and remove them with a spoon if necessary.

ג Meanwhile, heat olive oil in a pan on medium-high heat. And half of the onion, the meat, cumin, salt and pepper. Break up the chunks of meat and cook until browned.

ד Remove the meat from the pan and set aside.

ה Add the other half of the onion, the red pepper and carrot. Cook the veggies for a few minutes on high heat until browned but not cooked all the way through, so they still have a nice crunch.

ו *FOR THE TAHINI:*
Add the raw tahini to a small bowl with the lemon juice. Gradually mix in water until it reaches a smooth consistency. Some brands of tahini are thicker than other, so adjust the water accordingly. Season with salt to taste.

ז Drizzle tahini on the eggplant. Scoop some meat on top, followed by the cooked veggies, and more tahini.

The Best Brisket

Jamie wrote the book on Brisket. Brisket 101 was published in 2017 and featured on the TODAY Show. When it comes to brisket you don't want to risk it - so try this Best Brisket recipe and your splurge for this "buttery" cut will be worth it.

Serves 6

4 lb (1.8 kg) brisket
2 tablespoons oil
2 onions, sliced
6 cloves garlic, peeled
6 small carrots, 3 grated and 3 peeled
2 tablespoons tomato paste
2 teaspoons salt
½ teaspoons black pepper
1 tablespoon paprika
Pinch cayenne pepper
1 cup red wine
2 cups chicken stock
¼ cup brown sugar
2 tablespoons white vinegar
6 + stalks celery
1 bunch parsley
6 sprigs thyme
3 sprigs rosemary

א Preheat oven to 300°F / 150°C.

ב Heat oil in a pot on medium heat. Once hot, add the onions and stir occasionally until golden, about 15 minutes. Add the garlic, grated carrots, tomato paste and spices (salt, pepper, paprika and cayenne pepper). Stir and cook for 5 more minutes.

ג Add the red wine, chicken stock, brown sugar and vinegar. Stir well to scrape up the caramelized flavor from the bottom of the pan. Remove from heat.

ד Place the meat in a baking dish and carefully pour the sauce (from the pot) on top.

ה Place the celery and the 3 peeled carrots into the dish around the meat. Cover with aluminum foil and bake for 4 hours (or 1 hour per pound of meat).

ו Allow the brisket to cool and remove it from the dish. Slice against the grain with a sharp knife. After the meat is sliced, place it back into the dish and reheat before serving.

TIP
If you refrigerate the brisket before slicing, it will be much easier to slice when cold.

Cholent

Jews from around the world have developed unique versions of slow-cooked Shabbat stews. For this Ashkenazi version, you better grab your fiddle and dancing shoes. This cholent is going to take you back to the 1800s. To recreate the flavors of our ancestors, we used simple ingredients that were available back in the "shtetl" markets of Eastern Europe.

Serves 8

2 medium potatoes, peeled and chopped

1 onion, chopped

1½ lbs (700 g) stew meat, chuck or any fatty cut

4 garlic cloves, chopped

½ cup of barley

1 cup of mixed beans, kidney, pinto, navy

2 tablespoons sugar

2 teaspoons salt

½ teaspoon pepper

3 cups chicken broth

א In a slow cooker or an oven-proof pot, evenly layer the potatoes, onion, meat, garlic, barley and beans. Sprinkle the sugar, salt and pepper all over the top. Add 3 cups of chicken stock. If the chicken stock doesn't cover the ingredients, add a little water.

ב Place in the oven on 200°F / 90°C for at least 12 hours (or in a slow cooker on low).

Orisa

This Shabbat treat from Morocco is packed with flavor. It's typically started on Friday afternoon and served for Shabbat lunch. The flavorful combination of the meat with the garlicky, paprika-soaked, sweet potatoes is unlike anything in Western cooking. Sephardic Shabbat dishes almost always include eggs, called "huevos haminados", which turn brown after cooking at a low temperature for a long time.

Serves 6-8

⅓ cup olive oil
2 onions, chopped
1½ lbs (680 g) stew meat, chuck or any fatty cut
1½ cups barley
1 tablespoon sweet paprika
2 tablespoons brown sugar
1½ teaspoons salt
8 garlic cloves, whole peeled
2½ cups water
2 large sweet potatoes, cut into chunks
Eggs, one per person

א Heat olive oil in an oven-proof pot on medium heat. Once hot, add the onions. Stir occasionally until onions are soft, about 10 minutes.

ב Add the meat, barley (or rice), paprika, brown sugar, salt, and garlic. Mix and cook for 2 minutes.

ג Pour in the water and place the sweet potatoes and eggs on top.

ד To serve the orisa that day, cover and cook on low heat until the meat is soft, about 1½ hours. To serve for lunch the following day, place in the oven on 200°F / 90°C for 12 to 16 hours.

ה Peel the eggs before serving and place back on top of the orisa.

Mafrum

The Libyan Jewish community dates back more than 2,000 years. In 2003, the last Jew of Libya left the country. This incredibly flavorful Jewish - Libyan dish throws us back in time.

Serves 8

5 potatoes
1 cup flour
2 eggs
2 tablespoons vegetable oil, for frying

MEAT FILLING
1 lb (450 g) ground beef
½ cup parsley, chopped
2 eggs
½ large onion, chopped
⅓ cup breadcrumbs
¼ teaspoon cinnamon
¼ teaspoon cumin
2 teaspoons paprika
1 teaspoon salt
½ teaspoon black pepper

SAUCE
1 tablespoon vegetable oil
1 small onion, chopped
2 cloves garlic, chopped
2 tablespoons paprika
⅓ cup tomato paste
2 cups water
3 tomatoes, chopped
1 teaspoon salt
½ teaspoon black pepper

א Peel the potatoes and cut into ½ inch (1¼ cm) thick slices. Cut into each slice of potato to make a V shape (see picture).

ב Place the sliced potatoes in a bowl of water to keep fresh.

ג Place flour in a shallow dish. And eggs, beaten in a second dish.

ד Mix all the meat filling ingredients in a bowl. Take golf-ball sized balls of the meat and stuff them into the potato slices.

ה Roll the stuffed potatoes in flour, then in the eggs.

ו Add 2 tablespoons of oil to a pan and fry the potatoes on medium heat until golden. Flip to fry on all sides.

ז For the sauce, add oil to a pot on medium heat. Use a pot that has a lid. Cook the onion, garlic and paprika for 2 minutes. Stir frequently so that the paprika doesn't burn. Stir in the water, tomato paste, chopped tomatoes, salt and pepper.

Add the fried potatoes, cover and cook on low heat for 45 mins. Serve with couscous.

Hassleback Salami

There's a selection of Jewish-American recipes that don't necessarily have a connection with traditional Jewish life. This epic party appetizer fits right into that category.

Serves 6 appetizer portions

14-16 oz (425 g) salami
½ cup apricot jam
½ tablespoon hot sauce
1 tablespoon maple syrup
1 tablespoon brown sugar

א Preheat the oven to 400°F / 200°C. Place two chopsticks on both sides of the salami (with plastic removed).

ב Cut thin slices about ⅛ inch thick. The chopsticks stop the knife from completely cutting through the salami.

ג Mix the apricot jam, hot sauce, maple syrup and brown sugar in a bowl.

ד Pour over salami. Make sure it gets in between the slices.

ה Bake for 45 minutes or until crisped to your liking. Every 15 minutes, remove it from the oven and scoop some of the sauce onto the salami. That keeps it nice and juicy.

ו To serve, place on a platter with a knife so people can help themselves. Set a dish of mustard on the side.

▶ watch video

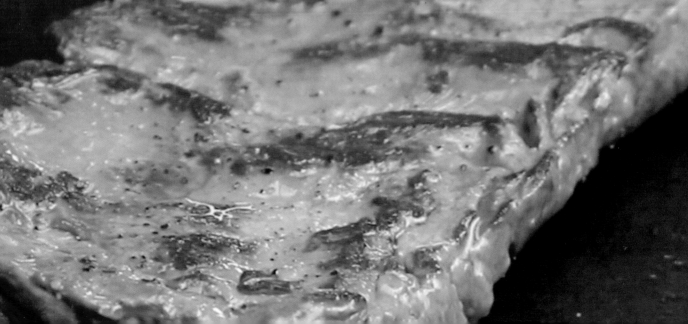

Steak-Stuffed Pita Fajita

Serves 6

6 pitas
1 lb (½ kg) skirt steak
2 tablespoons
    vegetable oil
1 small onion, chopped
1 small red bell pepper,
    sliced
1 small yellow bell
    pepper, sliced
1 small green bell
    pepper, sliced

SALAD
1 cup chopped parsley
2 cloves garlic, chopped
2 tomatoes, chopped
1 tablespoon olive oil
Juice of ½ lemon
Salt and pepper

DON'T FORGET
Tahini
Israeli pickles
Harissa/schug (spicy
    chili paste)

א Heat 1 tablespoon of oil in a skillet on high heat.

ב Rub steak with salt and pepper on both sides.

ג When the pan is very hot, carefully place the steak. Cook for 3 minutes without touching, then flip and cook for 3 minutes on the other side. Set the steak aside to rest for 5 minutes. Slice it against the grain' into strips (this makes the steak more tender).

ד Add more oil to the pan if there isn't any left. Add onions and peppers. Cook until veggies are caramelized but still crunchy, about 7 minutes.

ה For the salad, mix the parsley, garlic, tomatoes, olive oil, lemon juice, salt and pepper.

ו Slice each pita at the top and open it up with your fingers. Stuff it with tons of tahini, vegetables / salad, steak, pickles, schug (spicy chili paste).

▶ watch video

HOLIDAYS

חגים

[Hag-eem] – with a hard h

APPLE CHALLAH BREAD PUDDING

APPLE HONEY CAKE

CRISPY POTATO LATKES

CHEESY SWEET POTATO LATKES

SUFGANIYOT IN A BAG

FIJUELAS

ABIGAIL'S PEANUT BUTTER &
	CHOCOLATE HAMANTASCHEN

CHOCOLATE MATZAH CRUNCH

PIZZA-BREI

MATZAH LASAGNA

MOUFLETA FOR THE MIMOUNA
	PARTY

OREO CHEESECAKE

Apple Challah Bread Pudding

Serves 6-8

3 large eggs
2 cups non-dairy milk
1½ teaspoons cinnamon
1 teaspoons vanilla
½ large challah
1 tablespoon vegan
  butter
1½ tablespoons honey
2 Granny Smith apples,
  cored and chopped
½ cup pomegranate
  seeds (optional)

א Preheat oven to 350°F / 175°C.

ב In a large bowl, whisk the eggs, milk, cinnamon and vanilla. Add challah and soak for 30 minutes. This gives the bread its delicous custard-like texture.

ג In a pan, melt the butter on a medium-high heat. Add the honey and apples. Mix. Cook for about 5 minutes until the apples start to caramelize. Remove from heat, add the pomegranate seeds (optional) and mix.

ד Add the challah mixture to a greased 8 by 8 inch baking dish and spread evenly. Pour the apple mixture on top and spread.

ה Bake for 40 minutes, or until browned on top. Serve with a drizzle of honey or maple syrup and garnish with fresh pomegranate seeds.

▶ **watch video**

Rosh Hashana

Makes: 2 cakes

3 cups flour
1 teaspoon baking
   powder
1 teaspoon baking soda
1 teaspoon kosher salt
¼ cup white sugar
½ cup brown sugar
1 cup vegetable oil
¾ cup honey
2 large eggs
1 teaspoon vanilla
1 cup apple or orange
   juice
1 Granny Smith apple,
   peeled and sliced

א Preheat oven to 325°F / 160°C.

ב Mix the flour, baking powder, baking soda and salt in a large bowl.

ג Add everything else except the apples and mix again.

ד Grease 2 cake pans and place apple slices on the bottom. Pour some of the batter, then another layer of apples and finally the remaining batter. Place any remaining apple slices on top. The batter should fill halfway to the top of the pan. This cake rises a lot!

ה Bake for 50 minutes or until you can insert a knife into the center of the cake and remove it clean. Let the cakes to cool for 10 minutes, then flip them out of the pans.

Apple Honey Cake

Crispy Potato Latkes

{ Hanukkah }

Makes: 24 latkes

3 large potatoes, peeled
1 small onion, peeled
2 eggs
3 tablespoons flour
½ teaspoon salt
½ teaspoon black pepper
Oil, for frying

TOPPING
Applesauce
Sour cream

א Grate the potatoes and the onion using a hand grater or food processor with the grater attachment.

ב Place the grated potatoes and onion in a cloth and squeeze out all the liquid. This is the trick for making the latkes extra crispy, so make sure to squeeze really well.

ג Add the potatoes and the onion to a large bowl along with the eggs, flour, salt and pepper. Mix well.

ד Pour oil into a wide pan so it coats the entire surface. Place on medium heat. Once the oil is hot, scoop a spoonful of the mixture and place in the pan. Press down with the back of the spoon or a spatula to make it flat. Fry for about 2 minutes on each side until crispy.

ה Place the cooked latkes on paper towels to soak up the excess oil. Keep in a warm oven until serving. Serve with applesauce and sour cream.

▶ watch video

Cheesy Sweet Potato Latkes

{ Hanukkah }

Makes: 12 latkes

2 large sweet potatoes, peeled
3 green onions, chopped
2 large eggs
3 tablespoons flour
½ teaspoon salt
½ teaspoon black pepper
4 oz (110g) cheese of your choice, shredded (we use mozzarella)
Oil, for frying

TOPPING
Sour cream
Green onion, chopped

א Grate the peeled sweet potatoes using a hand grater or with the grater attachment on a food processor.

ב Place the grated sweet potatoes in a kitchen towel. Squeeze out as much liquid as you can. Sweet potatoes are tough, so use your muscles! The more you squeeze, the crispier the latkes.

ג Mix the potatoes in a large bowl with the green onions, eggs, flour, salt and pepper.

ד Pour oil into a wide pan so it coats the entire surface. Place on medium-low heat. Place a spoonful of the mixture in the pan. Press it down with the back of the spoon. Place a pinch of shredded cheese on top. Place another spoonful of the mixture on top and press it down again with the back of the spoon. Cook on each side for 5-7 minutes. If the latkes are burning at 5 minutes, turn the heat down a little.

ה Place the cooked sweet potato latkes on paper towels to drain the excess oil. Keep in a warm oven until serving. Serve with sour cream and chopped green onion.

▶ watch video

Hanukkah

Makes: 12 doughnuts

1 large egg
1½ tablespoons canola oil + more for deep-frying
2¼ teaspoons active dry yeast (1 packet)
½ teaspoon vanilla extract
3 tablespoons sugar
Pinch of salt
¾ cup warm water
3 cups all-purpose flour
1-2 cups of strawberry jelly
Powdered sugar

▶ watch video

א In a gallon-sized ziplock bag, add the egg, oil, yeast, vanilla, sugar, salt and warm water. Zip and shake to mix. Add the flour. Zip the bag and squeeze to mix the ingredients and knead the dough for about 5 minutes.

ב Place the bag in a bowl of very warm water to rise for 30 minutes.

ג Remove the dough from the bag and shape it into a cylinder. Cut the dough into 12 even pieces and roll each one on the table into a smooth ball. Place each ball of dough on a floured surface. Leave plenty of space between them since they double in size. Cover with a towel and allow the doughnuts to rise for 45 minutes.

ד Fill a large pot with 2 inches (5 cm) of oil and bring to 350°F/175°C. If you don't have a thermometer, then set the flame to medium heat and add the first doughnut. It should bubble and float to the top. Using a spatula, gently transfer some of the doughnuts into the oil. Cook for about 2 minutes on each side until golden. If the oil is too hot, it will turn brown in less than two minutes and the inside will remain uncooked, so adjust the heat accordingly.

ה Remove and set on paper towels.

ו With a squeeze tube or piping bag, squeeze jelly into the top of the doughnuts. Dust with powdered sugar.

Sufganiyot in a Bag

These crispy sugar-coated pastries are eaten on Purim and after fasting on Yom Kippur. Tunisians call these "deblas" and others call them "fazuelos". Apparently this dessert's name is a touchy subject in North African countries.

Makes: 12 pastries

2 large eggs
1 teaspoon baking powder
½ teaspoon salt
1 tablespoon sugar
2 tablespoons canola oil
1 tablespoon water
1½ cups flour

For the syrup:
1 cup sugar
1 cup water
1 tablespoon honey
1 tablespoon lemon juice

א Mix the eggs, baking powder, salt, sugar, oil and water in a large bowl. Gradually add the flour and mix until the dough is smooth (you can use your hands). Add more flour, 1 tablespoon at a time if the dough feels too wet to work with.

ב Sprinkle flour on the counter. Using a rolling pin or a pasta maker, roll the dough out as this as you possibly can. Cut into 1 inch wide strips.

ג Fill a frying pan with ½ inch of oil. Place on high heat for 2 minutes, then decrease the heat to low.

ד Now for the tricky part. Insert one strip of dough in between the prongs of a fork (see photos). While holding the long end, dip the fork into the oil and let it fry for several seconds until crispy. Twist the fork, rolling the dough so that a new part is exposed to the oil. Keep twisting until golden all the way around. Remove and let the fijuelas drain on paper towels.

ה For the syrup, heat the sugar, water, honey and lemon juice in a saucepan on medium heat. Stir until dissolved then simmer for 5 minutes. Individually dip each cooked fijuela into the syrup pan and tilt the pan so the syrup covers the fijuela completely.

▶ watch video

Fijuelas

Abigail's Peanut Butter & Chocolate Hamantaschen

"These are my favorite because they have my two favorite things in them. Chocolate AND peanut butter. Oh, and the rainbow sprinkles."
- Abigail, 9 years old, said in her adorable British acccent.

Makes: 20

8 tablespoons butter, softened
2 tablespoon sugar
4 tablespoons nutella
2 cups flour
2 tablespoons water
Peanut butter, sweetened (or Nutella)
Rainbow sprinkles

א Preheat the oven to 350°F / 175°C. Add the butter and sugar to a bowl. Mix until fluffy.

ב Add the Nutella. Mix.

ג Add the flour. Mix until it becomes a powder.

ד Add water one teaspoon of water one at a time, while mixing with your hands, until a dough forms.

ה Then squeeze into a ball with your hands.

ו Place the dough on a big sheet of plastic wrap. Place another piece of plastic over the dough. Roll the dough to ¼ inch thickness (½ cm) with a rolling pin. Remove the top sheet of plastic and cut 3 inch (7½ cm) circles with a cup.

ז Remove excess dough and transfer circles to a lined baking sheet. Repeat with the extra dough.

ח Place a teaspoon (no more than that) of peanut butter or Nutella in the center, fold the 3 sides tightly, top with rainbow sprinkles and bake for 15 minutes.

▶ watch video

TIP
Tip: if you put too much filling, they might open up in the oven.

Chocolate Matzah Crunch

Passover

Serves 8

4-5 sheets of matzah
1 cup butter
1 cup brown sugar
1 cup chocolate chips

TOPPING IDEAS
Sea salt
Sliced almonds
Crushed pretzels

א Preheat oven to 350°F / 175°C.

ב Cover a tray with baking paper. Fill the tray with the matzah sheets, breaking them to fit the entire tray.

ג Melt butter and brown sugar in a pot over medium heat. Stir constantly and bring to a boil. Boil for 3 minutes, stirring often.

ד Pour the toffee over the matzah and spread evenly with a spatula.

ה Bake for 10-15 minutes. Keep an eye on it and don't let it burn.

ו While the matzah is still hot, sprinkle the chocolate chips on top and let it sit for 5 minutes. Spread the chocolate with a spatula. Then sprinkle your favorite crazy toppings. Once it comes to room temperature, place it in the freezer for 30 minutes.

ז Cut into smaller pieces and place them in an airtight container. Store in the refrigerator or freezer and serve cold (the chocolate is less messy when cold).

▶ **watch video**

zza-Brei

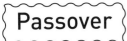

This twist on the classic "matzo brei" is a fun addition to the old-school Passover recipe list.

Passover

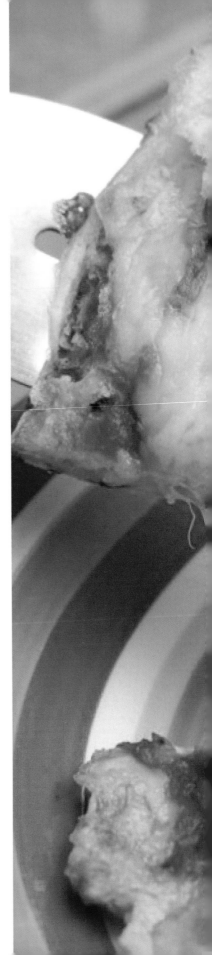

Serves 2

2 sheets matzah
4 large eggs
Salt & pepper
1 tablespoon butter

4 tablespoons pizza sauce
½ cup mozzarella, shredded

א Soak the matzah in water for 30 seconds. Remove and shake off the excess water.

ב Scramble the eggs in a bowl with the salt and pepper.

ג Melt the butter in a frying pan on a medium heat. Break the matzah into chunky pieces and add it into the pan. Pour in the egg mixture. Flatten the eggs and matzah with a spatula. Cover and cook on low heat for 5 minutes.

ד Remove the cover, then flip the matzah pancake onto a plate. Add it back into the pan so the cooked side is facing up. Spread the tomato sauce on top. Sprinkle the mozzarella along with other favorite toppings. Cover and cook on low heat for a few more minutes, until the cheese is melted.

watch video

Matzah Lasagna

Passover

Serves 4-6

1 tablespoon olive oil
½ onion, chopped
½ bell pepper, chopped
3 cloves of garlic, chopped
1 zucchini (1½ cups), sliced
28 oz (800g) tomato sauce
Salt and pepper to taste
Small bunch of fresh basil
3 sheets of matzah
12 oz (300g) ricotta cheese,
   shredded
12 oz (300g) mozzarella
   cheese, shredded
4 oz (110g) shredded
   Parmesan cheese,
   shredded

א Preheat oven to 350°F / 175°C. Heat olive oil on medium heat in a large pan. Cook the onions and pepper until the onions become soft, about 10 minutes.

ב Add the garlic and zucchini. Cook for 3 minutes, stirring occasionally. Pour in a jar of your favorite tomato sauce and toss in some fresh basil. Remove from heat then add salt and pepper to taste.

ג Spread a thin layer of the tomato sauce on the bottom of a 9 x 9 inch baking dish.

ד Soak 3 sheets of matzah for 30 seconds in warm water. Shake off the excess water. Place one sheet of matzah on top of the sauce. If you're using a wider dish, you might need more matzah to fill the shape. Spread ⅓ of the ricotta on the matzah, followed by ⅓ of the mozzarella and ⅓ of the Parmesan. Spread another layer of sauce then repeat.

ה Bake for 35 to 45 minutes until crisped to your preference.

▶ watch video

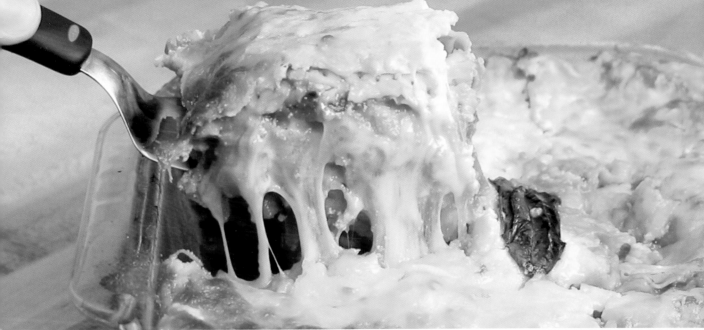

On the night when Passover ends, Moroccan Jewish families celebrate with a special Mimouna party. Every Mimouna party needs two things: people shouting "kulululu!" and freshly cooked moufleta. Traditionally, Mimouna was a time when Muslim neighbors brought gifts of fresh flowers, milk and fruit to their Jewish freinds in Morocco. Tables were decorated with gold coins and fresh fish to symbolize prosperity and fertility. It was a time for seeing friends and celebrating. In Israel today, Moroccans still celebrate Mimouna, and it's a party that everyone wants to be invited to!

Passover

Makes: about 20

3½ cups (18 ounces) flour
1 teaspoon sugar
1 teaspoon kosher salt
2 teaspoons yeast
1½ cups warm water
½ cup vegetable oil
Butter and honey, for
    serving

א Mix the flour, salt, sugar and yeast in a large bowl. Add the water and mix until a dough forms. Knead until very smooth, about 3-5 minutes.

ב Using your thumb and forefinger, pinch a small ball of dough and place on a large tray covered with oil. Flip the dough balls in the oil so they don't dry out. Repeat with all the dough. Cover the dough and let it rest for 20 minutes.

ג Starting with the dough that was rolled first, take one ball and place it on a smooth surface. With well-oiled hands, flatten and press the dough into a very thin circle. If it tears easily, let it rest for 10 more minutes then try again.

ד Place the first moufleta in a large frying pan on medium-low heat. Cook for about 3 minutes while you flatten the second moufleta. When the first one is golden brown, flip it over. This is the only moufleta that is cooked on both sides! Moufleta are cooked in a stack which keeps them hot until serving. Place the second moufleta on top and flip the stack. While the second moufleta is cooking, flatten the third moufleta. Place the third moufleta on top then flip. Repeat until the stack is too heavy to flip, then start a new stack.

ה Serve hot with butter and drizzle with honey. Celebrate the mimouna with dried fruits and nuts.

▶ watch video

Moufleta
for the Mimouna Party

Oreo Crust Cheesecake

Israel is known as the land of "milk and honey," so it's no surprise that there is a holiday during which we eat tons of cheesy food.

Serves 8

CRUST

40 Oreos, crushed, or 3½ cups of graham cracker crumbs

8 tablespoons butter, melted

CHEESECAKE

24 oz (680g) cream cheese

1½ cups sugar

4 large eggs, separated

1 tablespoon lemon juice

1 teaspoon vanilla

א Preheat the oven to 325°F/160° C

ב For the crust, either grind the Oreos (or graham crackers) in a good processor or crush them in a plastic bag with a rolling pin.

ג Mix the crumbs with the melted butter. Add the mixture to a 9 inch springform pan. Using a measuring cup, press the crumbs firmly against the bottom and sides of the pan to form a crust.

ד In a bowl, use a hand mixer to combine the cream cheese, sugar, egg yolks, lemon juice, and vanilla.

ה In another bowl, use a hand mixer to mix egg whites until they become stiff and fluffy (that's called "stiff peaks").

ו Scoop the egg whites into the cream cheeese mixture and gently mix with a spatula. Pour into the pan and use the spatula to flatten the top.

ז Bake for 35 minutes. Turn off the oven and let it sit for 1 hour. Don't open the oven door.

ח Freeze the cheesecake for at least 3 hours. Remove it from the pan while frozen.

DESSERTS

TAHINI COOKIES

DAIRY-FREE CHOCOLATE CHIP

   COOKIES

 CHOCOLATE RUGELACH IN A BAG

MALABI (ROSEWATER PUDDING)

COCONUT MERINGUE MONSTER

   COOKIES

CHOCOLATE BABKA IN A BAG

BAKLAVA

on the outside and chewy on the inside, these cookies fit perfectly into our theme of modern Israeli cooking. Dunk them into a cup of strong black coffee, change your name to Yuval, and wham! Suddenly you're the most Israeli person you know.

Makes: about 12

⅔ **cup raw tahini**
1 teaspoon vanilla
1 egg
⅔ **cup sugar**
1 teaspoon baking powder
Pinch salt
½ **cup flour**

א Preheat the oven to 350°F / 175°C.

ב Mix all ingredients except the flour in a bowl.

ג Add the flour and mix until it looks crumbly.

ד Using your hands, take a small handful of the crumbly dough and squeeze it into a ball. Then flatten it between your palms and place on a parchment lined baking sheet.

ה Use your thumb to make an indent in the center of each cookie and place an almond there. You can also use a fork to flatten each ball and make pretty lines.

ו Bake for 10 minutes. Give these cookies plenty of time to cool before eating. They stay fresh for several days. Delicious with coffee and tea!

▶ **watch video**

Tahini Cookies

Dairy-Free Chocolate Chip Cookies

These cookies are dairy-free, so they are Kosher to eat after meat meals. We make them almost every Shabbat!

Makes: 16 cookies

1½ cups flour
½ teaspoon baking soda
½ cup sugar
½ cup brown sugar
½ teaspoon salt
1 large egg
½ cup oil
1 teaspoon vanilla
½ cup non-dairy chocolate chips

א Preheat the oven to 350°F / 175°C.

ב In a large bowl, mix the flour, baking soda, sugar, brown sugar and salt with a fork.

ג In a separate small bowl mix the egg, oil and vanilla with a fork. Add the egg mixture to the dry ingredients and mix well. Add chocolate chips then mix again.

ד With your hands, squeeze the dough into balls then flatten into disks. Placed on a non-stick baking sheet. Bake for 12 minutes.

ה Allow to cool completely before digging in so they don't crumble!

Chocolate Rugelach in a Bag

Most American-style rugelach are crisp. These Israeli-style rugelach are reminiscent of those from the markets in Jerusalem- soft, chocolatey and gooey.

Makes: 30 rugelach

DOUGH

1 large egg + 1 more for basting

¼ cup melted butter (or canola oil)

⅓ cup warm milk (or water)

½ teaspoon vanilla extract

2¼ teaspoons active dry yeast (1 packet)

2½ tablespoons sugar

½ teaspoon salt

1¾ cups flour

FILLING

⅓ cup cocoa powder

½ cup butter, softened

3 tablespoons honey

SYRUP

½ cup water

½ cup sugar

▶ watch video

א In a gallon-sized ziplock bag, add one egg, melted butter (or oil), milk (or water), vanilla, yeast, sugar, salt and flour. Squish and knead the bag for 5 minutes until the dough is evenly mixed. Place the bag in a bowl of very warm water for 45 minutes.

ב Preheat the oven to 350°F / 175°C. For the filling, mix the cocoa powder, softened butter, and honey in a bowl. If the butter is too hard, you can melt it. *If you melt it, stick it in the refrigerator before you spread it on the dough.

ג Separate the dough into 3 even balls. To ensure that the dough doesn't stick to the table when rolling, keep your work surface dusted with flour. Roll out each ball until the dough is super thin. Make sure it's not stuck to the table. If it is, then dust the dough with flour and flip it over. Place a plate on the dough, cut around it and remove excess dough.

ד Spread ¼ of the filling. Cut into 8 slices, like a pizza. Separate each slice and roll tightly. *You need to separate the slices so they don't get covered in chocolate on the outside from the other slices. Place each rugelach on a non-stick baking tray.

ה Brush with a beaten egg and bake until golden, about 15-20 minutes.

ו Meanwhile, make the glaze by combining water and sugar in a saucepan on medium heat. Stir until the sugar melts. When the rugelach are done baking, brush all of the glaze onto the rugelach, which will soak it up.

Malabi
(Rosewater Pudding)

▶ watch video

Legend has it that Malabi was served to a Turkish general named Al-Muhallab by a Persian chef in the 17th century. He liked it so much that he named it after himself. Today, malabi is a popular dessert in Israel and at Turkish Jewish weddings, to celebrate a sweet and flowery future.

Serves 4

PUDDING
1½ cups milk
⅓ cup sugar
3 tablespoons cornstarch
½ cup cold water
½ tablespoon rosewater
½ cup heavy cream

SYRUP
¼ cup sugar
¼ cup pomegranate juice
½ teaspoon rosewater

TOPPINGS
Shredded coconut
Chopped pistachios

א Mix the milk and sugar in a pot on medium heat until dissolved.

ב Mix the cornstarch and water in a separate bowl.

ג When the milk comes to a simmer, turn the heat to medium-low and add the cornstarch mixture. Cook for 5 minutes, stirring often.

ד Remove from heat. Add the rosewater and heavy cream. Whisk to mix and remove any clumps. Scoop the mixture into small cups and refrigerate for several hours until solid (or enjoy hot- which is perfect for the winter).

ה For the syrup, mix all the ingredients over medium heat. Mix the sugar to dissolve and bring to a boil. Allow it to bubble for 3 minutes, stirring occasionally. Allow to cool completely before pouring on the malabi.

ו Sprinkle coconut and chopped pistachios before serving.

Coconut Meringue Monster Cookies

Makes: 8 big meringues

1¾ cup white sugar
5 large egg whites
½ teaspoon cocoa powder
Pinch of salt
¾ cup unsweetened
shredded coconut
3 oz (80g) dark chocolate

TOPPINGS
2 oz (50g) dark chocolate,
 grated
½ teaspoon cocoa powder

א Preheat oven to 400°F / 200°C.

ב Pour sugar onto a parchment lined baking sheet. Bake the sugar for 7 minutes.

ג Meanwhile, using an electric mixer, beat the egg whites on medium speed until foamy. Once the sugar is hot, reduce the oven temperature to 225°F / 110° C. Remove the sugar from the oven. Then carefully grasp the ends of the parchment paper and pinch one side to make a 'scooper'. Pour half of the sugar into the whipped egg whites. Continue to whip the eggs for 30 seconds then add the second half of the sugar. Continue to mix on medium-high speed until meringue can hokd a peak.

ד Sift the cocoa powder across the top of the meringue. Sprinkle the coconut and salt across the top too. Gently fold the meringue with a spatula two or three times. You don't want to mix it, just fold it into layers.

ה Prepare a parchment-lined baking sheet. With a spatula, scoop 8 meringues. Use a spoon to gently push the meringue off the spatula onto the tray. Use the spoon to make a pretty-looking peak on each meringue.

ו For the toppings, sift some cocoa powder and sprinkle grated chocolate.

ח Bake for 1½ hours. The inside should be gooey and delicious.

Chocolate Babka in a Bag

Makes: 1

DOUGH
2¼ teaspoons active dry yeast

⅓ cup warm water

1 egg

½ teaspoon orange zest

2 tablespoons sugar

⅛ teaspoon salt

⅛ teaspoon vanilla

2 tablespoons vegan butter, softened

1¾ cups flour

FILLING
13 oz. (370g) Nutella

⅓ cup semi-sweet chocolate chips

SYRUP
3 tablespoons water

3 tablespoons sugar

▶ watch video

א Open a large zip-top bag and place it on the counter. Add the yeast, water, egg, orange zest, sugar, salt, vanilla and vegan butter. Close the bag and squeeze to mix thoroughly.

Open the bag and add the flour. Squeeze and knead until the dough is a somewhat even consistency. Place the bag in a bowl of warm water to rise for 1 hour.

ב Remove the dough and place on a well-floured surface. Roll out the dough into a large rectangle.

ה Spread nutella on the dough, avoiding 1 inch around the edges. Sprinkle the chocolate chips evenly.

ו Starting from one of the long edges of the dough, roll up the dough into a rope. Cut the dough in half down the middle of the rope. Place one strand on top of the other to create a large X, then twist the remaining ends.

ז Place in a greased 8-inch loaf pan, cover and place in a warm part of the kitchen to rise for one hour or until doubled in size.

ח Preheat the oven to 350°F / 175°C.

ט Bake for 40 minutes.

י Remove the babka from the oven then place a small sauce pan on medium heat. Add the water and sugar then bring to a simmer. Once sugar is dissolved, brush the syrup on top of the babka.

Baklava

Makes: 30 pieces

**1 package filo dough
(usually 1lb / 500g)**
**1 cup canola oil or 2 sticks
melted butter**
**3.5 oz (100g) chopped
pistachios for garnish**

FILLING
**1 lb (450g) finely chopped
almonds or mixed nuts**
¼ cup white sugar
1 teaspoon cinnamon
¼ teaspoon cardamom

SYRUP
1 cup water
1 cup sugar
½ cup honey
2 tablespoons lemon juice

א Defrost the filo dough according to the instructions on the package. Trust them. They know what's up when it comes to defrosting dough.

ב Preheat the oven to 350°F / 175°C. For the filling, mix the nuts, sugar, cinnamon and cardamom in a bowl. Cover the stack of filo dough with plastic wrap and a towel while you aren't working with it. This prevents it from drying out (which happens quickly).

ג Brush the inside of a wide baking dish with oil or butter. Place one sheet of filo dough in the dish. Oil the top of that sheet. Repeat with 7 more sheets, bushing each one. Scoop half of the nuts into the dish and spread evenly.

ד Place 8 more sheets of dough, brushing each one with oil or butter between the layers. Add the second half of the nuts and spread evenly. On top of that goes 8 more sheets of filo dough, brushing each one, and finally, brush the top layer.

ה Make 4 cuts down the pan lengthwise. Then make diagonal cuts across the pan. Sprinkle the top of the dough with some cold water, which prevents the filo from curling. Bake for 30-40 minutes until the top is golden.

ו To make the syrup, add the sugar, water, honey and lemon juice to a small pot on medium heat. Stir until the sugar dissolves then simmer for 5 minutes. Remove from heat and allow it to cool.

ז Once the baklava is removed from the oven, pour the cooled syrup on top. Let it rest for 4 hours to soak up the liquid.

▶ watch video

It takes a village...

...to write a cookbook.

This book is lucky number 7 but only because I had a LOT of help from my friends.

The first and most prominent thank you goes to the entire (and extended) Attias family for birthing, nurturing and growing this brand from day one and every day thereafter. With a very special thank you to Mrs. Cindy Attias aka Chef C along with all the grandparents and generations of family whose recipes, lives and travels have inspired the food on these pages.

A tremendous thank you to my work family, the Kauftheil, Magerman, Weiss and Genger families – you are the pillars on which this brand and business stand.

And my final thank you, for now, (until I get it into my head that the world needs another cookbook) is to my family, the Mendelovici (Tauber, Tal, Zuckerman) and Geller mishpachas -- who show up each and every day, with prayers and support, belief and faith, inspiration and motivation, patience and ready plates — without which I could never do what I do, for the last 15 years.

Nachum, Bracha Miriam, Rochel Naami, Yaakov Yosef, Avraham Yitzchak (AY), Noa (Noeeee!) and Shaulie Dovid you bring me joy and purpose and nachas that knows no bounds.

And to YOU who put the U in community, whether we are family from Facebook, Instagram, email, the website or because you have just stumbled upon this book...

We love, appreciate and cherish sharing good food and a piece of our collective soul with you.

With love from Israel,
Jamie

About the Authors

Dana Attias

Having spent most of her life moving between London and Israel, Dana has both a cheeky British side and an outgoing Israeli side. After receiving her degree in finance (with honors) from IDC Herzliya, Dana travelled the world and soaked up its flavor. Her favorite dishes are: fried fish in Spain, pasta in Italy, curry in India, tacos in Mexico and of course, shakshuka in Israel. Dana's vision for Jewlish by Jamie is what makes it so diverse. FUN FACT: The garment in the photo above is embroidered entirely with gold-thread. It belonged to Dana's great-grandmother and every bride in her family wears it at their Henna party (a Moroccan pre-wedding celebration).

Jacob Attias

Jacob moved from Cleveland, Ohio to Israel where he found the two loves of his life, Israeli cuisine and Dana. His love for food began during the years he worked at his mom's catering company, schlepping stacks of plates, smoking salmon and baking bread. In Israel, Jacob founded a digital media company that grew to 5 million monthly users and $5m yearly revenue. Jewlish by Jamie is the perfect recipe to blend Jacob's passion for business and food.

Jewish food and lifestyle expert and author of seven best- selling cookbooks, Jamie Geller is famous for sharing Jewish comfort food with fans worldwide. Jamie's global media brand includes her website JamieGeller.com, which features over 10,000 recipes, and the viral @JewlishbyJamie how-to videos with almost 1 BILLION views. Jamie also hosts the Chanukah Cooking Special with Jamie Geller on PBS and Create TV, is a regular on the TODAY Show and has been featured on ABC, NBC, CBS, Martha Stewart Living Radio, Forbes, Family Circle, Cosmopolitan and the Chicago Tribune. Jamie and her husband live in Israel with their six children ky"h — their favorite 'activity' is family dinner. Jamie loves nothing more than sharing Jewish comfort food with friends, family and a worldwide community of food enthusiasts.